1   *There are many ways of completing this question. The specimen completion below would receive full marks.*   (15)

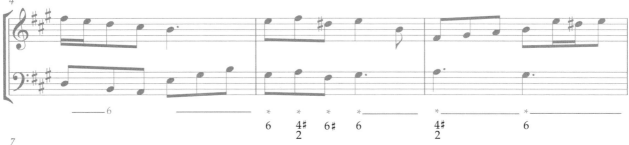

2   *There are many ways of completing this question. The specimen completion below would receive full marks.*   (15)

Source (adapted): J. S. Bach, Chorale 'Es ist gewißlich an der Zeit'

3   *There are many ways of completing this question. Either of the specimen completions below would receive full marks.*   (20)

EITHER

(a)   *Source (adapted): Mendelssohn, 'Es weiß und rät es doch keiner', Op. 99 No. 6*

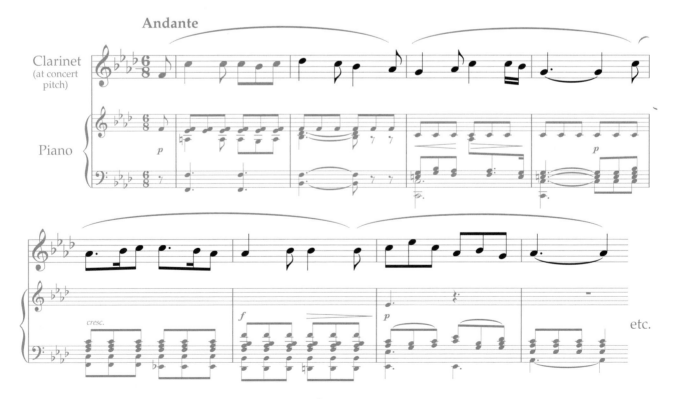

Grade

7

4.50

Music Theory Past Papers 2016

Model Answers

ABRSM Grade 7

Welcome to ABRSM's *Music Theory Past Papers 2016 Model Answers*, Grade 7. These answers are a useful resource for students and teachers preparing for ABRSM theory exams and should be used alongside the relevant published theory past papers.

All the answers in this booklet would receive full marks but not all possible answers have been included for practicable reasons. In these cases other reasonable alternatives may also be awarded full marks. For composition-style questions only one example of the many possible answers is given.

For more information on how theory papers are marked and some general advice on taking theory exams, please refer to the Music Theory Grade 7 web page: www.abrsm.org/theory7.

Using these answers

- Answers are given in the same order and, where possible, in the same layout as in the exam papers, making it easy to match answer to question.

- Where it is necessary to show the answer on a stave, the original stave is printed in grey with the answer shown in black, for example:

- Alternative answers are shown in one of three ways:

    1. separated by an oblique stroke (/), for example: V⁷c / V⁷c major

    2. by using *or*, for example:

    3. by using boxes where the definition of a phrase consists of two or more terms. Correct answers may be constructed by selecting any one option from each box, as in this example:

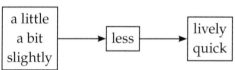

- American note names, for example half note and quarter note, are accepted but have not been included in the answers as they are not used in the exam papers.

- Where the source of an excerpt is not identified in full in the question paper, it is given at the start of the answer to enable candidates to consult the original. The specimen answers do not necessarily follow the composer's original.

- Extended roman and basic roman numerals are used in answers that require chord identification.

- The old-style crotchet rest is accepted as a valid alternative to the modern symbol .

- Sometimes the clef, key and time signature of the relevant bar(s) are included for added clarity, for example:

© 2017 by The Associated Board of the Royal Schools of Music
Published by ABRSM (Publishing) Ltd, a wholly owned subsidiary of ABRSM
Cover by Kate Benjamin & Andy Potts
Printed in England by Halstan & Co. Ltd, Amersham, Bucks, on materials from sustainable sources

OR

(b) *The given opening is printed in grey in order to distinguish it from the completion. Candidates do not have to use the given opening in their answer, and may instead choose to write their own.*

violin

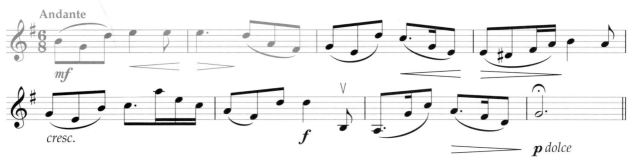

4 (a) (i)   17–18   (2)
        (ii) major 13th / compound major 6th   (2)

     (b) Bar 11   V⁷c / V⁷c major   }Key   D minor   (7)
          Bar 19   Neapolitan 6th / ♭IIb / ♭IIb major

     (c) *All possible answers are shown on the extract reproduced below. For full marks, candidates need to identify only one example of each answer.*

          B   Bar   8   (2)
          C   Bar(s) 2–3 / 7   (2)
          D   Bar   8   (2)
          E   Bars   11–12   (2)
          F   Bar   4   (2)

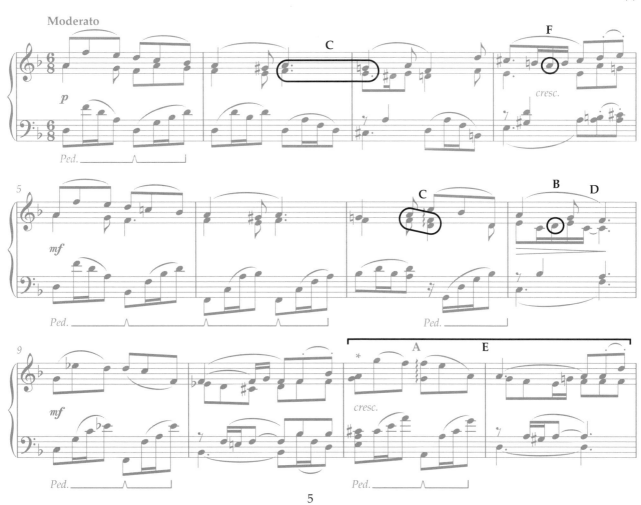

(d)   (i)   true   (2)

    (ii)   false   (2)

5   (a)   roll / drum roll / rapid reiteration of the same note   (2)

           with mutes / muted   (2)

           keep with the soloist / with the soloist   (2)

Walton, Violin Concerto (transposed)

(b)   (i)   Clarinets 1 2   (2)

    (ii)   Horns   1 2   3 4   (4)

(c)   (i)   4   (2)

    (ii)   double basses; harp   (2)

    (iii) harp; third horn   (2)

    (iv) F♯   (1)

(d)   1   minor 3rd   (2)

    2   perfect 4th   (2)

(e)   true   (2)

Theory Paper Grade 7   2016   B
Model Answers

1   *There are many ways of completing this question. The specimen completion below would receive full marks.*   (15)

2   *There are many ways of completing this question. The specimen completion below would receive full marks.*   (15)
     Source (adapted): J. S. Bach Chorale 'Hilf, Herr Jesu, laß gelingen'

3 *There are many ways of completing this question. Either of the specimen completions below would receive full marks.* (20)

EITHER

(a) *Source (adapted): Berlioz, 'Oh! par pitié' from L'enfance du Christ, Op. 25, Part 3*

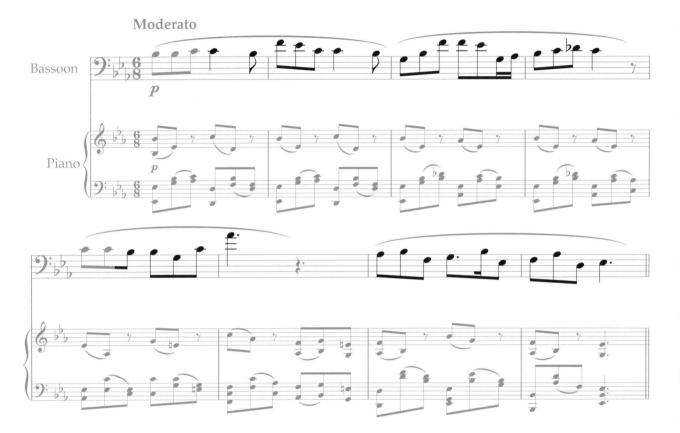

OR

(b) *The given opening is printed in grey in order to distinguish it from the completion, but candidates must include the opening in their answer.*

cello

4   *Source: Schubert, Der Jüngling am Bache, D. 192*

    (a)   at a moderate speed / moderately   (2)

    (b)   Bar 1   diminished 7th / vii°^{7}a / VII^{7}a diminished
                Bar 21   ii°^{7}b / II^{7}b diminished / iv^{6}a / IV^{6}a minor   }Key   F minor   (7)

    (c)   *All possible answers are shown on the extract reproduced below. For full marks, candidates need to identify*
         only one example of each answer.

B	Bars	11–12	(2)
C	Bar	10	(2)
D	Bar	18	(2)
E	Bar	17 / 19	(2)
F	Bars	14–16	(2)

(d) (i)   3 / 5 / 19   (2)
    (ii) perfect octave / perfect 8th / perfect 8ve   (2)

(e)   <u>1750–1850</u>   (1)

    late Classical or early Romantic style / expressive style   (1)

5   (a)   roll / drum roll / rapid reiteration of the same note   (2)
          tremolo / rapid reiteration of the same note / rapidly alternating bow strokes   (2)
          very held back   (2)

(b) (i)   Horns   (4)

    (ii) Clarinets   (2)

(c) 1   major 13th / compound major 6th   (2)
     2   minor 9th / compound minor 2nd   (2)

(d) (i)   first bassoon; first clarinet; cor anglais   (3)
    (ii) double basses; third bassoon   (2)

(e) (i)   false   (2)
    (ii) true   (2)

10

Theory Paper Grade 7   2016   C
Model Answers

1   *There are many ways of completing this question. The specimen completion below would receive full marks.*   (15)

2   *There are many ways of completing this question. The specimen completion below would receive full marks.*   (15)
Source (adapted): Mozart, Piano Sonata in D, K. 284, third movement

3 *There are many ways of completing this question. Either of the specimen completions below would receive full marks.* (20)

EITHER

(a) *Source (adapted): Bridge, 'Country Dance' from Four Short Pieces*

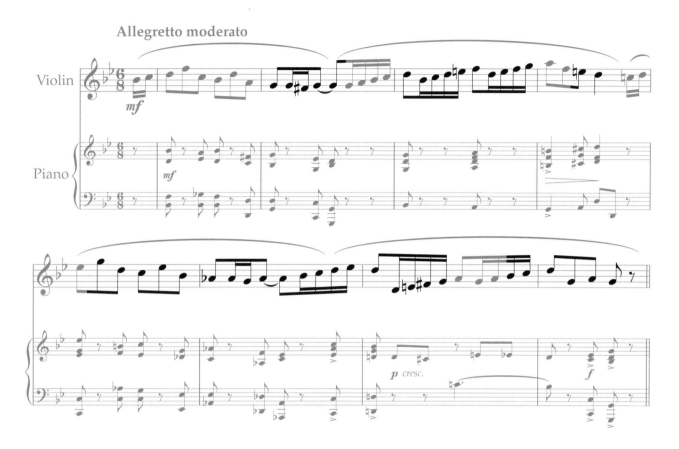

OR

(b) *The given opening is printed in grey in order to distinguish it from the completion, but candidates must include the opening in their answer.*

flute

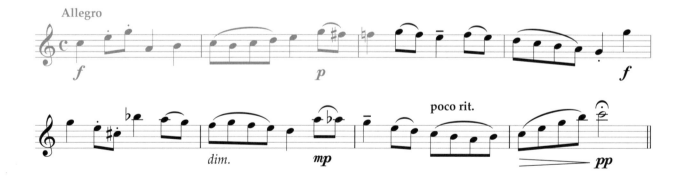

4 *Source: Telemann, No. 6 from Six Sonatinas, TWV 41: F1, second movement*

(a)

(3)

(b) Bar 7   ii°⁷b / II⁷b diminished / iv⁶a / IV⁶a minor   Key   A major / A minor   (4)
     Bar 13   Neapolitan 6th / ♭IIb / ♭IIb major   (3)

(c) *All possible answers are shown on the extract reproduced below. For full marks, candidates need to identify only one example of each answer.*

       B   Bars   11–12   (2)
       C   Bar   10 / 12   (2)
       D   Bar   15   (2)

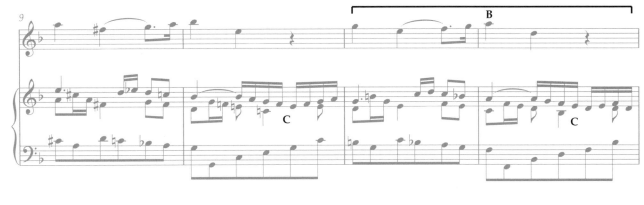

(d) (i)   false   (2)
     (ii)   true   (2)
     (iii) true   (2)

(e)   1700–1800   (1)

     One mark will be awarded (up to a maximum of two marks) for each correct reference to the following:
     use of 'keyboard' rather than piano / harmony / texture / lack of dynamics /   (2)
          use of ornaments

5   (a) (i)   double basses; cellos   (2)
         (ii)   7   (2)
         (iii) 3–4 / 4   (2)

R. Strauss, Symphony Op. 12 (transposed)

     (b) (i)   Horns   (4)

13

(ii) Clarinets 1 2   (2)

(c)   1   major 6th   (2)

      2   minor 3rd   (2)

      3   augmented 11th / compound augmented 4th   (2)

(d)   Bassoon 1   (3)

(e)   (i)   false   (2)

      (ii)   true   (2)

Theory Paper Grade 7   2016   S
Model Answers

1   *There are many ways of completing this question. The specimen completion below would receive full marks.*   (15)

2   *There are many ways of completing this question. The specimen completion below would receive full marks.*   (15)
  Source (adapted): J. S. Bach, Chorale 'Mach's mit mir, Gott, nach deiner Güt'

3   *There are many ways of completing this question. Either of the specimen completions below would receive full marks.*   (20)

EITHER

(a) *Source (adapted): Schubert, 'Das Fischermädchen' from Schwanengesang, D. 957*

OR

(b) *The given opening is printed in grey in order to distinguish it from the completion, but candidates must include the opening in their answer.*

clarinet

4   *Source: Mozart, Piano Sonata in F, K. 280, second movement*

(a)   Bar 2   ii°⁷b /II⁷b diminished / iv⁶a / IV⁶a minor   Key   F minor   (4)
       Bar 15   diminished 7th   (3)

(b)   (5)

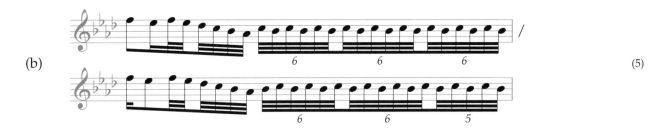

(c)   *One mark will be awarded (up to a maximum of three marks) for each correct reference to the following:*
       minor to major tonality / lack of dissonance / thinning of texture /   (3)
       unbroken movement in left-hand part / less sustained right-hand melody /
       no use of ♩.♪♪ rhythm / pause in bar 8

(d)   *One mark will be awarded (up to a maximum of two marks) for each correct reference to the following:*
       Similarities   harmonic underlay / melodic shape / dynamics   (2)

       One mark will be awarded (up to a maximum of two marks) for each correct reference to the following:
       Differences   bars 22–24 an octave lower / phrase extended in bar 24 /   (2)
                       appoggiatura in bar 24

(e)   *All possible answers are shown on the extract reproduced opposite. For full marks, candidates need to identify only one example of each answer.*
       B   Bar   19   (2)
       C   Bars   12–13   (2)
       D   Bar   19 / 20   (2)

16

5 (a) playful / joking (2)
on the G string (2)
with the bow / bowed (2)

(b) (i)

Rachmaninoff, *Caprice bohémien* (transposed)

(4)

(ii) Horns (3)

© Copyright 1896 by Hawkes & Son (London) Ltd
Reproduced by permission of Boosey & Hawkes Music Publishers Ltd.

(c) **1** minor 10th / compound minor 3rd (2)
2 perfect 5th (2)

(d) 6 (2)

(e) (i) true (2)
(ii) false (2)
(iii) true (2)

Music Theory Past Papers 2016 Model Answers

Model answers for four past papers from ABRSM's 2016 Theory exams for Grade 7

Key features:

- a list of correct answers where appropriate
- a selection of likely options where the answer can be expressed in a variety of ways
- a single exemplar where a composition-style answer is required

Support material for ABRSM Music Theory exams

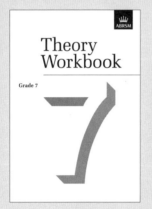

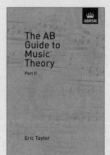

**Supporting the teaching and learning of music
in partnership with the Royal Schools of Music**

Royal Academy of Music | Royal College of Music
Royal Northern College of Music | Royal Conservatoire of Scotland

www.abrsm.org   f facebook.com/abrsm

🐦 @abrsm   ▶ ABRSM YouTube

ISBN 978-1-84849-819-8

ABRSM